MW00416850

NEWLYWEDS

JEFF ATWOOD

HARVEST HOUSE PUBLISHERS
EUGENE, OREGON

Cover and interior design by Studio Gearbox
Cover photo © Olga Milagros / Shutterstock

Published in partnership with Brentwood Studios.
BrentwoodStudios.net

Need to Know for Newlyweds
Copyright © 2020 by Jeff Atwood
Published by Harvest House Publishers
Eugene, Oregon 97408
www.harvesthousepublishers.com

ISBN 978-0-7369-8115-6 (hardcover)
ISBN 978-0-7369-8116-3 (eBook)

Printed in the United States of America

20 21 22 23 24 25 26 27 28 / VP / 10 9 8 7 6 5 4 3 2 1

TO ANNETTE
MY BRIDE, FOREVER AND
FOR ALWAYS

INTRODUCTION

Congratulations on your wedding. You are embarking on some of the most exciting days in your life. With just a handful of "I do's," you magically created a whole new family. Enjoy every moment. I wish you the very best as you enter this amazing new journey.

We are forever thankful to Brent and Laurie Lamb. So much of our relationship was shaped by yours. Someday we hope to be just like you. ("You can't see me; I'm camouflaged.")

Also, thanks to Kendall and Chase Owens, Tayler and David Johnston, and Kali and Will Henke for your review and input on early versions of this book.

Special thanks to Kendal and CJ Gaston for trusting me to officiate your wedding. It was in preparing for that day that many of the thoughts in these pages came to life.

NEED TO KNOW

If you are giving this book as a gift to a friend or family member, you are aware that they need to know a lot more than what is contained in these pages. Please take a minute to share advice you think the recipients of this book need to know to have a successful marriage.

The same applies to you, the reader. Please take a moment to write down some ideas or experiences you want to remember so you can share them with other newlyweds.

_____

_____

_____

_____

_____

_____

_____

HERE'S A SIMPLE
QUESTION TO ASK YOURSELF
BEFORE YOU SLEEP:
DID I MAKE LIFE BETTER OR
WORSE FOR MY SPOUSE TODAY?
THE ANSWER SHOULD
HELP SHAPE TOMORROW.

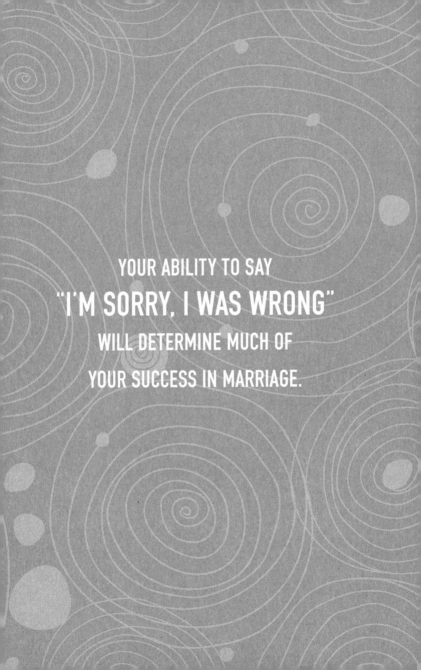

YOUR ABILITY TO SAY
"I'M SORRY, I WAS WRONG"
WILL DETERMINE MUCH OF
YOUR SUCCESS IN MARRIAGE.

WHEN YOU ARE
TEMPTED TO ROLL YOUR EYES
AT YOUR SPOUSE'S CHOICES,
REMEMBER THAT
YOU
ARE ONE OF THOSE CHOICES.

RESPECT YOUR SPOUSE'S
FAMILY TRADITIONS.
YES, THEY MIGHT BE WEIRD,
BUT REMEMBER,
THAT WEIRDNESS HELPED SHAPE
THE PERSON YOU'RE CHOOSING
TO SPEND YOUR LIFE WITH.

BE CONTENT.

YOU DON'T ALWAYS NEED MORE

OR SHINIER OR NEWER OR IMPROVED STUFF.

IF YOU'RE IN THE HABIT OF ALWAYS

CHASING SOMETHING,

GIVE IT UP.

GET IN THE RHYTHM OF TALKING (NOT TEXTING)

AT LEAST ONCE DURING THE DAY. NO ONE IS TOO BUSY FOR A 30-SECOND CHECK-IN. THERE IS SOMETHING REASSURING ABOUT HEARING THE VOICE OF THE ONE YOU LOVE MOST IN LIFE.

IT'S OKAY TO FEEL
SCARED SOMETIMES.
EVERYONE DOES.
BEING MARRIED BRINGS
LOTS OF NEW THINGS.

TELL YOUR SPOUSE

YOU LOVE THEM.

EVERY DAY.

WHETHER YOU FEEL LIKE IT

OR NOT AT THE MOMENT.

**DON'T REFER
TO EACH OTHER AS
"MY BETTER HALF."**
NOT ONLY IS IT UNTRUE,
IT'S JUST PLAIN WEIRD.

SOMETIMES YOU JUST
NEED TO BE QUIET.
DON'T TRY TO GET THE LAST WORD
OR INSIST ON BEING RIGHT.
KEEPING YOUR MOUTH SHUT IS
A GREAT WAY TO AVOID SAYING
ANYTHING MEAN OR HURTFUL.

MAKE YOUR FAVORITE

WEDDING GIFT YOUR

"GO TO" GIFT

FOR EVERY WEDDING YOU ATTEND.

MARRIAGE DOES NOT MAKE
TWO IMPERFECT PEOPLE
PERFECT; BUT IT DOES TURN
TWO IMPERFECT PEOPLE INTO A
PERFECTLY FINE FAMILY.

REGULARLY GET TOGETHER
WITH COUPLES WHO HAVE
BEEN MARRIED FOR A LONG TIME
AND LEARN FROM THEM.
ASK QUESTIONS, LIKE
"WHAT WERE YOUR HARDEST TIMES,
AND HOW DID YOU SURVIVE THEM?"
OR "WHAT WAS THE MOST
IMPORTANT THING YOU LEARNED
FROM YOUR SPOUSE?"

THE PHRASE "MY FAMILY" NOW APPLIES PRIMARILY TO YOU AND YOUR SPOUSE.

DECISIONS MUST NOW INCLUDE

YOUR NEW FAMILY FIRST

AND YOUR OLD FAMILY SECOND.

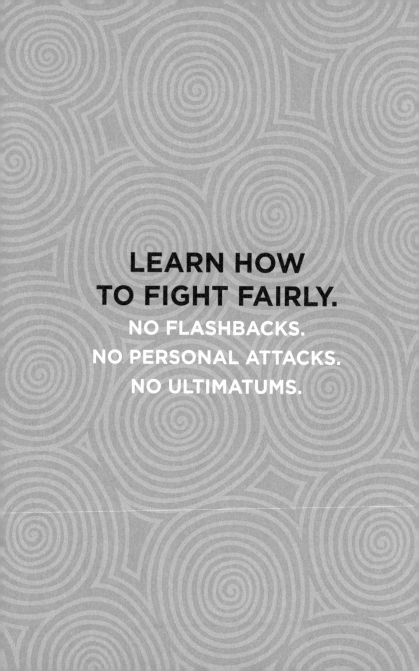

LEARN HOW TO FIGHT FAIRLY.

NO FLASHBACKS.
NO PERSONAL ATTACKS.
NO ULTIMATUMS.

THE ONLY
"YOURS" AND "MINE"
SHOULD BE
UNDERWEAR DRAWERS.

UNKIND WORDS HAVE
A LONG SHELF LIFE.
THEY CRAWL INTO DEEP,
DARK CORNERS OF OUR PSYCHES
WHERE THEY ARE NEARLY IMPOSSIBLE
TO EXTRACT OR ELIMINATE.
ALWAYS BE MINDFUL
OF WHAT YOU SAY.

MAKE THE WORLD A BETTER PLACE
TOGETHER.
WHEN YOU VOLUNTEER,
GIVE, OR SERVE TOGETHER,
YOU IMPROVE NOT ONLY THE WORLD
BUT ALSO YOUR RELATIONSHIP.

IF YOU JUST CAN'T REACH
A DECISION ON A MATTER,
FLIP A COIN.
HALF THE TIME IT WILL
TURN OUT THE WAY
YOU WANTED.

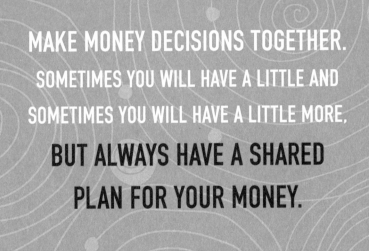

MAKE MONEY DECISIONS TOGETHER.
SOMETIMES YOU WILL HAVE A LITTLE AND
SOMETIMES YOU WILL HAVE A LITTLE MORE,
BUT ALWAYS HAVE A SHARED
PLAN FOR YOUR MONEY.

WHENEVER YOU CAN,
DO THINGS INSTEAD
OF BUYING THINGS.
GOOD MEMORIES FUEL A LONG,
HAPPY JOURNEY.

GIVE YOUR SPOUSE'S INTERESTS OR HOBBIES A TRY. YOU CAN LEARN A LOT ABOUT PEOPLE BY LEARNING WHAT THEY LIKE TO DO.

THERE ARE NO SECRETS.
**WHAT YOU KNOW,
HE OR SHE MUST KNOW**
(EXCEPT CHRISTMAS PRESENTS, OF COURSE).

AGREE ON HOUSEHOLD CHORES,
LIKE LAUNDRY, CLEANING, COOKING,
OR MOWING THE GRASS.
DON'T EXPECT THE OTHER
PERSON TO DO SOMETHING
JUST BECAUSE THAT'S THE WAY IT
WAS DONE WHERE YOU GREW UP.

**THINK LONG AND HARD
BEFORE SAYING
"I WISH YOU WOULD..."
THAT'S A DANGEROUS WAY
TO START A CONVERSATION.**

ONE OF THE MOST IMPORTANT
THINGS YOU CAN DO IS TO
HELP YOUR SPOUSE BE THE
BEST VERSION OF THEMSELVES.
YOUR ROLE IS NOT TO MAKE THEM BETTER,
BUT TO HELP THEM BETTER THEMSELVES.

SOMETIMES FRUSTRATION
NEEDS A LITTLE
BREATHING ROOM.

YOUR LIFE WILL INEVITABLY
INCLUDE UNPLANNED,
HILARIOUS MOMENTS.
MAKE SURE YOU
REMEMBER THESE MOMENTS
BY TAKING PICTURES
AND WRITING THINGS DOWN.
YOU (AND YOUR CHILDREN) WILL
TREASURE THESE MEMORIES.

GIVE YOURSELF
PERMISSION
TO LEAN ON
YOUR PARTNER.

MAKE SURE YOU AGREE ON HOLIDAY CELEBRATIONS.

PERHAPS ONE OF YOU GREW UP WITH RENTED UNICORNS AND CATERED BUFFETS AT YOUR BIRTHDAY PARTIES, WHILE THE OTHER WAS ACCUSTOMED TO CAKE AND CANDLES AND A CARD. APPRECIATE EACH OTHER'S CONTEXT AND WORK TOGETHER TO CHOOSE THE RIGHT WAY FOR YOUR NEW FAMILY TO CELEBRATE.

ALL THE WONDERFUL
FAMILY TRADITIONS YOU GREW
UP WITH WERE STARTED
BY SOMEONE SOMEWHERE.
NOW IS YOUR CHANCE TO
START YOUR
OWN TRADITIONS.

MAKE SURE YOU AGREE
ON YOUR DEFINITIONS OF
THRIFTINESS AND EXTRAVAGANCE.

WHEN YOU START
TO GET SIDEWAYS
WITH EACH OTHER
AFTER THE WEDDING,
REMEMBER HOW YOU
FELT ABOUT AND ACTED
TOWARD EACH OTHER
BEFORE THE WEDDING.
DO THAT AGAIN.

COUNT TO TEN
(OR TEN THOUSAND IF NEED BE)
INSTEAD OF CALLING SOMEONE TO
COMPLAIN ABOUT YOUR SPOUSE.
FEW THINGS ARE WORSE THAN
SPEAKING POORLY ABOUT
YOUR HUSBAND OR WIFE.

NEVER EVER,
EVER USE
"I'M LEAVING"
AS A THREAT.
NEVER.
EVER.

NO HOUSEGUESTS FOR MORE THAN TWO CONSECUTIVE NIGHTS DURING YOUR FIRST YEAR OF MARRIAGE.

(ESPECIALLY THE SUPER COOL UNCLE
WHO IS BETWEEN JOBS AGAIN
AND JUST NEEDS A PLACE TO CRASH.)

MONEY GOES IN
ONE ACCOUNT.
AGREE ON WHERE IT
GOES FROM THERE.

FIND THINGS THAT BRING ORDER TO YOUR LIFE.

SIMPLE THINGS, LIKE TACO TUESDAY OR SATURDAY MORNING LAUNDRY, CAN BRING RHYTHM TO YOUR NEW FAMILY.

SET A SUNDAY EVENING
"CALENDAR MEETING"
TO REVIEW PLANS FOR UPCOMING WEEKS.
YOU CAN REDUCE
UNPLEASANT SURPRISES
AND PRIORITIZE THINGS TOGETHER.

GET COMFORTABLE
WITH THE FACT THAT
NO MATTER HOW WELL YOU THINK
YOU KNOW YOUR SPOUSE,
YOU HAVE A LOT MORE TO LEARN.
AND THAT'S AWESOME.
YOU'RE IN THIS
FOR THE LONG HAUL.

YOU WON'T AGREE ON
EVERYTHING, BUT MAKE
SURE YOU HAVE A
GOOD FOUNDATION
ON THE BIG THREE
(MONEY, RELIGION, AND KIDS)
FROM DAY ONE.

HUMILITY IS UNDERRATED.
FIND WAYS TO PUT
YOUR SPOUSE'S NEEDS
ABOVE YOUR OWN
AS OFTEN AS YOU CAN.

DON'T WITHHOLD SEX
AS A PUNISHMENT.
LEAVE THE FIGHT IN THE DEN.
OR THE KITCHEN.
OR THE CAR.
SEX IS AN EXPRESSION OF LOVE;
FIGHTS DON'T NEGATE LOVE.

DETERMINE A
SPENDING THRESHOLD THAT
YOU WON'T EXCEED WITHOUT
TALKING WITH YOUR SPOUSE.
NOT EVEN FOR
GIFTS OR SURPRISES
(OR ITEMS ON CLEARANCE).

PETS SHOULD NEVER BE SURPRISE GIFTS. ESPECIALLY AFTER A FIGHT.

"HEY, I'D LIKE YOU TO MEET OUR NEW DOG. I NAMED HIM 'SORRY I FORGOT TO TELL YOU ABOUT MY GOLF TRIP WITH THE BOYS ON YOUR MOM'S BIRTHDAY.'"

FIND THE RIGHT
WAYS TO DISAGREE.
FOCUS ON THE ISSUES—
DON'T MAKE
IT PERSONAL.

FIND OUT WHETHER YOUR
SPOUSE LIKES TO TALK
**BEFORE OR AFTER
MORNING COFFEE.**
EMBRACE THEIR STYLE,
OR YOU WILL BOTH
START EVERY DAY
BEING GRUMPY.

IF YOU HAVE
MORE THAN ONE
BATHROOM IN YOUR HOME,
AGREE ON A
"POOPY POTTY."

#COURTESYFLUSH

AGREE ON ONE
KIND OF TOOTHPASTE.
YOUR TEETH REALLY
AREN'T THAT DIFFERENT.
(THIS IS BOTH A PRACTICAL CONSIDERATION
AND A RELATIONAL METAPHOR.)

SEE PREVIOUS, AND THEN
SOLVE THIS AGE-OLD CONUNDRUM:
SQUEEZE FROM THE MIDDLE
OR ROLL UP FROM THE BOTTOM?
(AGAIN, THIS IS BOTH
A PRAGMATIC ISSUE AND
A PROBLEM-SOLVING EXERCISE.)

LEARN HOW TO SAY
WHAT'S BOTHERING YOU
WHEN IT'S BOTHERING YOU.
IF YOU'RE ALL FUSSY OR GRUMPY
AND YOUR SPOUSE ASKS WHAT'S WRONG,
AVOID REPLYING "NOTHING" AND SKULKING AWAY.
YOUR SPOUSE WILL FEEL LIKE YOU JUST
PUSHED THEM AWAY. BECAUSE YOU DID.

ANSWER THE PHONE
WHEN YOUR SPOUSE CALLS.
IF HE OR SHE NEEDS
OR WANTS TO TALK
ABOUT SOMETHING,
THAT MAKES IT A PRIORITY.

COMPROMISE

IS NOT ALWAYS

YOUR SPOUSE AGREEING

WITH WHAT YOU WANT.

GO ON DATES.

(IF I NEED TO CLARIFY
THIS MUST BE RESTRICTED
TO YOUR SPOUSE,
THIS MAY NOT BE THE
RIGHT BOOK FOR YOU.)

BE THE
FIRST TO SAY
"I'M SORRY."

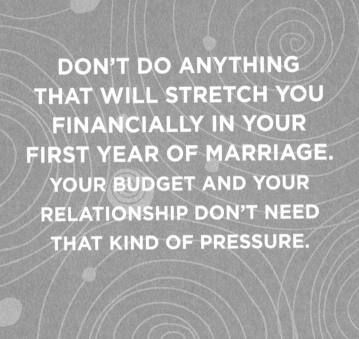

DON'T DO ANYTHING
THAT WILL STRETCH YOU
FINANCIALLY IN YOUR
FIRST YEAR OF MARRIAGE.
YOUR BUDGET AND YOUR
RELATIONSHIP DON'T NEED
THAT KIND OF PRESSURE.

DEVELOP COMMON INTERESTS.
AND "COMMON" DOES NOT MEAN
"ARE YOU COMING TO MY
KICKBALL GAME ON THURSDAY?"
IT MEANS THE ACTIVITY
(WHICH MAY BE NEW TO BOTH OF YOU)
ACTIVELY INVOLVES YOU BOTH.

HONESTY IS THE
NOT JUST THE
BEST POLICY;
IT IS THE
ONLY POLICY.

PIZZA IS THE PERFECT MARRIAGE FOOD. YOU CAN AGREE AND DISAGREE ABOUT WHAT TO EAT AT THE SAME TIME.

NEVER EVER, EVER
PUT DOWN YOUR SPOUSE

IN FRONT OF FRIENDS OR FAMILY,

REGARDLESS OF THE REASON

FOR YOUR FRUSTRATION.

YOU'RE ON THE SAME TEAM;

DON'T EVER THROW HIM

OR HER UNDER THE BUS.

RECORD YOUR BEST
MOMENTS IN A JOURNAL
OR A PHOTO GALLERY.
MAKE SURE IT'S EASIER TO
REMEMBER THE GOOD TIMES
THAN THE BAD TIMES.

BEGIN TALKING ABOUT HOLIDAY PLANS EARLY. "MY FAMILY HAS ALWAYS GONE TO AUNT EDNA'S ON CHRISTMAS EVE" IS NOT A REASON TO ASSUME THAT TRADITION SHOULD CONTINUE. MAKE HOLIDAY PLANS TOGETHER— AS EARLY AS POSSIBLE— AND COMMUNICATE THEM TO EVERYONE INVOLVED.

DON'T WAIT TO TRAVEL.
OR TO SAY I'M SORRY.
OR TO DO ANYTHING.
THERE ARE NO GUARANTEES
ABOUT NEXT YEAR OR NEXT WEEK
OR EVEN YOUR NEXT BREATH.
DON'T BE THE PERSON
WHO HAS TO SAY
"ONE DAY WE WERE GOING TO..."

AGREE ON WHAT IT
MEANS TO BE ON TIME AND
WHAT IT MEANS TO BE LATE.
WHAT YOU CONSIDER ON TIME,
YOUR SPOUSE MIGHT DEEM RUDELY LATE.
OR WHAT YOU REGARD AS LATE,
YOUR SPOUSE MIGHT
CONSIDER CLOSE ENOUGH.

IGNORING PROBLEMS
DOES NOT MAKE THEM
GO AWAY.
IT ONLY MAKES THEM
TOUGHER TO SOLVE.

SHE IS NOT YOU.
HE IS NOT YOU.
YOUR NEW SPOUSE IS A LOT OF THINGS,
BUT CONTRARY TO THE ROMANTIC COMEDIES
YOU MAY HAVE SEEN, YOUR SPOUSE DOES NOT
FILL YOU OR FIX YOU OR COMPLETE YOU.
YOU WERE MADE BY GOD
TO BE JUST RIGHT.
YOU MUST CONTINUE TO BE YOU.

THE SILENT TREATMENT

ONLY WORKS WHEN...

OH, WAIT,

IT NEVER WORKS.

YOU HAVE TO TALK IT OUT.

AGREE ON WHAT A CLEAN HOUSE IS.

YOU MAY BE FINE AS LONG AS THERE ARE NO RODENTS IN THE PANTRY, WHILE YOUR SPOUSE EXPECTS THE HOUSE TO BE READY FOR A MAGAZINE PHOTO SHOOT. MAKE SURE YOU FIGURE OUT THAT MIDDLE GROUND.

HAVE THE
"WHERE DO YOU SEE US IN 25 YEARS?"
CONVERSATION. YOU LIKELY
WON'T BE IN THE SAME PLACE INITIALLY,
BUT IT'S HELPFUL IF YOU'RE AT LEAST
ON THE SAME CONTINENT.

SEE PREVIOUS,
AND THEN HAVE THE
SAME CONVERSATION
EVERY ANNIVERSARY.
THE MORE OFTEN
YOU LOOK AHEAD TOGETHER,
THE MORE LIKELY YOU WILL BE TO
END UP IN THE SAME PLACE.

MARRIAGE IS NOT
A DESTINATION;
IT IS A JOURNEY.
ENJOY EVERY STEP
ALONG THE WAY.

YOU'RE LIKELY TO EXPERIENCE
EVERYTHING YOU MENTIONED
IN YOUR WEDDING VOWS
(FOR RICHER, FOR POORER,
IN SICKNESS, IN HEALTH...).
IT'S NOT LIKE BINGO,
WHERE YOU WANT TO COVER THE CARD.
BUT STILL, JUST KNOWING
THOSE THINGS ARE COMING
CAN HELP YOU BE READY.

**NO ONE IS PERFECT.
NOT YOU. NOT HIM OR HER.
(AND CERTAINLY
NOT YOUR PARENTS
OR AN OLD BOYFRIEND
OR GIRLFRIEND.)
IT'S NOT FAIR TO
EXPECT PERFECTION
OF YOUR SPOUSE.**

BE ON THE SAME PAGE ABOUT KIDS.

BEGIN BY AGREEING ON WHETHER TO HAVE KIDS, HOW MANY, WHEN, AND SO ON. THEN REMEMBER THAT PLANS AND DREAMS CAN CHANGE.

THINGS WILL RARELY
TURN OUT HOW YOU PLANNED.
THE GOOD NEWS IS THAT MOST OF THE TIME,
LIFE TOGETHER WILL BE BETTER THAN
YOU IMAGINED. BE FLEXIBLE ENOUGH TO
ENJOY THE JOURNEY—AND TO LAUGH.

RELATIONSHIPS,
JUST LIKE PEOPLE,
ARE NEVER COMPLETE;
THEY ARE ALWAYS IN PROCESS.
**BOTH OF YOU WILL
ALWAYS BE CHANGING.**
TALK ABOUT THESE
CHANGES IN OUTLOOK
AND EXPECTATIONS
EARLY AND OFTEN.

FROM THE MOMENT
SOMEONE SAYS
"I NOW PRONOUNCE YOU..."
YOU HAVE A NEW FAMILY.
DON'T FORGET THAT.

THE PHRASE
"FOR EASIER AND FOR HARDER"
SHOULD BE ADDED
TO THE WEDDING VOWS.
YOU WILL HAVE BOTH.

**TAKE ADVANTAGE OF
YOUR NEWLYWED YEARS
TO TRAVEL AND EXPLORE.**
YOU PROBABLY HAVE LESS MONEY
THAN YOU WILL HAVE LATER,
BUT WITHOUT KIDS OR
ADDITIONAL CAREER
RESPONSIBILITIES,
YOU MAY HAVE MORE FREE TIME.
PUT IT TO GOOD USE.

TRY TO UNDERSTAND EACH OTHER'S "HISTORIC TIME COMMITMENTS." IF HE SPENDS MARCH MADNESS WEEKEND WITH BUDDIES OR SHE DOES A FOURTH OF JULY GIRLS' BEACH TRIP, YOU DON'T HAVE TO CHANGE THINGS. JUST MAKE SURE YOU'RE ON THE SAME PAGE ABOUT THEM.

DON'T BE THE ONE
WHO BUSTS THE BUDGET.
REMEMBER, IT'S NOT
"MY MONEY" OR "YOUR MONEY"
ANYMORE.
IT'S "OUR MONEY."

DO ALL YOU CAN TO AVOID DEBT.

LIKE AN ANCHOR ON A SHIP, IT CAN KEEP YOU STUCK IN ONE PLACE, UNABLE TO MOVE FORWARD IN MANY PARTS OF YOUR LIFE.

MARRIAGE IS LIKE MATH.
IT STARTS OUT EASY BUT GETS MORE
COMPLEX WITH MORE VARIABLES.
SEVEN YEARS IN,
YOU MAY FEEL LIKE YOU'RE DOING
COLLEGE-LEVEL CALCULUS EVERY DAY.
GET GOOD AT THE BASICS EARLY ON.

IN CASE YOU WONDERED, THESE ARE
THE BASICS FOR A GOOD MARRIAGE:
TELL THE TRUTH.
SAY "I'M SORRY."
TRUST GOD.
BE FLEXIBLE.
PRETTY MUCH EVERYTHING
ELSE IS GRAVY.

MASTER THE BASICS
OF WORKING ON
YOUR RELATIONSHIP.
THEN BEGIN WORKING TOGETHER
**TO MAKE THE WORLD
A BETTER PLACE.**

TAKE LOTS OF
PICTURES TOGETHER.

DON'T WORRY ABOUT
FILTERS OR HASHTAGS;
JUST GET PLENTY OF PICTURES OF
THE TWO OF YOU THAT MAKE YOU SMILE.
MEMORIES FEED THE SOUL AND
REFLECT YOUR LIFE TOGETHER.

IT'S IMPORTANT TO UNDERSTAND
WHAT'S IMPORTANT
TO YOUR SPOUSE.
YOU LIKELY WON'T ALWAYS AGREE
ON WHAT IS IMPORTANT;
JUST RECOGNIZE AND RESPECT
EACH OTHER'S PRIORITIES.

DON'T FEEL THE NEED
TO SHARE EVERY BIT OF
YOUR LIFE ON
SOCIAL MEDIA.
THE ONLY TRULY
IMPORTANT AUDIENCE
IS YOUR SPOUSE.

FIND A WAY
TO GIVE YOUR SPOUSE
ONE TRUE COMPLIMENT EVERY DAY.
IT DOESN'T HAVE TO BE BIG,
BUT IT DOES NEED TO BE REAL.

HAVE AN UNDERSTANDING
ABOUT WHAT CONSTITUTES "DAILY CHINA."
MAYBE OVERGENERALIZING A BIT HERE,
BUT MANY GUYS THINK
ALL FOOD CAN BE CONSUMED IN
STADIUM TUMBLERS AND GIANT CEREAL BOWLS.
GIRLS OFTEN DO NOT.
FIND THE HAPPY MEDIUM.

THERE WILL LIKELY COME A MOMENT DURING
THE FIRST FEW MONTHS OF MARRIAGE WHEN YOU
LOOK AT YOUR SPOUSE AND WONDER,
"WHAT WAS I THINKING?"
THIS MIGHT HELP.
JUST A FEW MONTHS AGO YOU WERE THINKING,
"THIS IS THE PERSON WHO WAS PUT ON
THIS EARTH FOR ME, AND I GET TO SPEND
MY WHOLE LIFE WITH HIM/HER."
SO WHEN YOU ASK YOURSELF
"WHAT WAS I THINKING?"
ANSWER THAT QUESTION THE WAY YOU WOULD
HAVE ANSWERED IT A FEW MONTHS EARLIER.

SEE PREVIOUS.
ANOTHER WAY TO
LOOK AT THE QUESTION
"WHAT WAS I THINKING"
IS TO ASK,
"WHAT WAS HE/SHE THINKING?"
THE TRUTH IS, LIVING WITH YOU IS
PROBABLY NO WALK IN THE PARK
RIGHT NOW EITHER.

THE SUM OF A
MARRIAGE IS ALWAYS 100,
BUT RARELY WILL IT BE AN EVEN
50/50 BALANCE.
SOMETIMES YOU CAN GIVE MORE;
AT OTHER TIMES YOU'LL NEED
YOUR SPOUSE TO BE STRONGER.
RARELY EXACTLY EVEN, BUT TOGETHER,
ALWAYS ENOUGH.

MAKE SURE YOU'VE HAD
THE BEDROOM TALK.
AIR TEMPERATURE,
TYPE OF BLANKETS,
TAUTNESS OF SHEETS...
AND THE OTHER STUFF TOO.

FIND THE THINGS
THAT MAKE YOU LAUGH
AND DO THEM A LOT.

DON'T EVER, EVER SAY
"YOU ALWAYS..."
OR "YOU NEVER..."
FIRST, IT'S MOST LIKELY NOT TRUE,
AND SECOND, THE ONLY REASON
YOU WOULD SAY IT
IS TO BE MEAN.
CHOOSE KINDNESS INSTEAD.

DEVELOP A HABIT OF
COMPLIMENTING YOUR SPOUSE
WHEN THEY'RE NOT AROUND.
SAYING GREAT THINGS ABOUT THEM
TO OTHERS IS A GREAT WAY TO
REMIND YOURSELF OF THEIR GREATNESS.

DON'T EVER
WEAR MATCHING CLOTHES.
YOU'LL THANK ME
WHEN YOU SEE THOSE PICTURES
20 YEARS FROM NOW.

MORE OFTEN THAN NOT, THE PHRASE
"YOU ARE SO SELFISH"
IS JUST A PASSIVE-AGGRESSIVE
WAY OF SAYING
"YOU AREN'T DOING WHAT I WANT,"
WHICH IS JUST ANOTHER WAY OF SAYING
"I AM SO SELFISH."

**SHARE EACH OTHER'S
USERNAMES AND PASSWORDS
FOR ALL ONLINE AND
SOCIAL MEDIA ACCOUNTS.**
NO SECRETS.

THERE ARE TWO KINDS
OF PEOPLE IN LIFE—
DECORATIVE-BED-PILLOW PEOPLE AND
NON-DECORATIVE-BED-PILLOW PEOPLE.
AGREE ON THE APPROPRIATE
NUMBER OF BED PILLOWS
BEFORE GOING SHOPPING.

DON'T DO ANYTHING
TO MAKE YOUR SPOUSE THINK
LESS OF THEMSELVES.
YOUR MISSION IS TO BUILD THEM UP,
NOT BRING THEM DOWN.
BE A LIFE GIVER,
NOT A LIFE SUCKER.

TAKE SOME TIME
EVERY NOW AND THEN
TO MARVEL AT THE FACT THAT
OF ALL THE PEOPLE IN THE UNIVERSE,
YOU'RE THE ONE WHO GETS TO
SPEND YOUR LIFE WITH YOUR SPOUSE.
TELL THEM HOW THANKFUL YOU ARE.

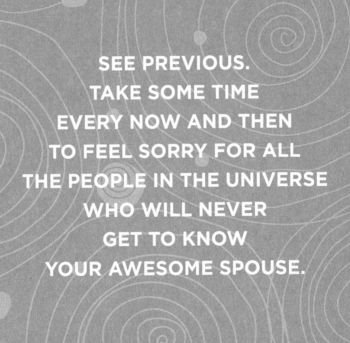

SEE PREVIOUS.
TAKE SOME TIME
EVERY NOW AND THEN
TO FEEL SORRY FOR ALL
THE PEOPLE IN THE UNIVERSE
WHO WILL NEVER
GET TO KNOW
YOUR AWESOME SPOUSE.

BIG DECISIONS
MUST BE UNANIMOUS.
WALK INTO EVERY NEW VENTURE
OR CHANGE *TOGETHER*.

TAKE TURNS PICKING THE RESTAURANT, MOVIE, OR TV SHOW.

DEAL WITH YOUR OWN FAMILY OF ORIGIN.
BE VERY CAUTIOUS ABOUT STICKING YOUR NOSE
INTO YOUR SPOUSE'S RELATIONSHIPS WITH THEIR
PARENTS, SIBLINGS, CRAZY AUNTS, AND SO ON.
IF A RELATIONSHIP IS TOXIC,
YOU MUST CERTAINLY SPEAK UP,
BUT WE ALL HAVE SOOO MUCH HISTORY
WITH OUR FAMILIES, IT'S OFTEN TOUGH
FOR A NEW FAMILY MEMBER
TO FULLY UNDERSTAND.

YOU WILL
MAKE MISTAKES,
BOTH TOGETHER
AND INDIVIDUALLY.
BE QUICK TO FORGIVE AND,
EQUALLY IMPORTANT, FORGET.

IF YOUR OPTIONS ARE
TO SAY SOMETHING MEAN
OR TO SAY NOTHING,
CHOOSE SAYING NOTHING.
EVERY SINGLE TIME.

PRAY FOR
ONE ANOTHER.
YOUR MARRIAGE IS BIGGER
THAN THE TWO OF YOU.

GO TO BED AT THE SAME TIME WHENEVER POSSIBLE. ADJUST YOUR SCHEDULE IF YOU NEED TO. NO ONE WANTS TO BE LONELY AT BEDTIME.

TRY NOT TO MAKE ANY BIG CHANGES
(OTHER THAN JUST BEING MARRIED)

FOR A YEAR.

IF YOU TRY TO BALANCE A NEW JOB,
A PREGNANCY, A HOME PURCHASE, DEBT,
OR A MOVE ACROSS THE COUNTRY
ON TOP OF THE NEW FAMILY DYNAMIC,
SOMETHING MAY COME TUMBLING DOWN.

KEEP IT SIMPLE.

WHEN YOU "WIN"
A DISAGREEMENT
AND THE DUST SETTLES,
DO YOU DO THE INTERNAL
SMIRKY VICTORY DANCE,
OR DO YOU OFFER GRACE
AND QUICKLY MOVE ON?
YOUR RESPONSE IS A PRETTY
GOOD BAROMETER FOR HOW YOU
FEEL ABOUT YOUR SPOUSE.

**DREAM BIG.
TOGETHER.**
SET DOWN YOUR PHONES.
TURN OFF THE TV.
LOOK ONE ANOTHER
IN THE EYE AND SAY,
"WHAT GREAT THINGS
CAN WE DO TOGETHER?"
THEN GET STARTED ON
ONE OF THOSE THINGS.

YOUR SPOUSE IS ALWAYS NUMBER ONE.

IN YOUR HEART.

IN YOUR MIND.

IN YOUR STORIES.

IN YOUR THOUGHTS.

IN YOUR TIME MANAGEMENT.

IN YOUR EVERYTHING.

NO TOPIC IS TOO BIG OR TOO LITTLE TO TALK ABOUT.

IT'S AMAZING WHAT HAPPENS WHEN YOU PUT FEELINGS OR IDEAS INTO WORDS AND SHARE THEM WITH YOUR SPOUSE.

EMPATHY GOES
A LONG WAY.
WHEN THINGS START TO GO
SIDEWAYS, TAKE A TWO-SECOND
TIMEOUT FROM YOUR OWN
PERSPECTIVE AND TRY
TO UNDERSTAND YOUR
SPOUSE'S POINT OF VIEW.

PLAN A COUPLE OF
INEXPENSIVE ROAD TRIPS.
CHEAPISH HOTELS, TACO BELL VALUE MEALS,
AND SHARED ICE CREAM BOUGHT WITH
THE CHANGE FROM THE CAR DASH.
VISIT YOUR STATE'S BIGGEST BALL OF TWINE OR
THE BIRTHPLACE OF A RANDOM UNKNOWN DUDE.
THE JOY IS NOT SO MUCH IN THE DESTINATION
BUT IN THE WEIRDNESS OF THE JOURNEY.

MAKE GROWN-UP
FINANCIAL DECISIONS EARLY.
RETIREMENT PLANNING, SAVING,
GIVING, AND LIFE INSURANCE
ARE ALL IMPORTANT.
INSTEAD OF SEEING THESE
AS HASSLES OR EXPENSES,
CELEBRATE THEM AS
RITES OF PASSAGE
FOR YOUR NEW FAMILY.

SOMETIME IN THE FIRST FEW
MONTHS OF MARRIAGE, YOUR SPOUSE
WILL DO SOMETHING YOU'VE NEVER NOTICED
BEFORE, LIKE A WEIRD LAUGH OR
A QUIRKY HABIT.
BUT NOW IT'S EVIDENTLY SOMETHING
THEY DO EVERY FIVE MINUTES.
GUESS WHAT? IT WASN'T A THING BEFORE,
AND IT DOESN'T HAVE TO BE A THING NOW.
SO JUST FOLLOW THE ADVICE OF
OUR FAVORITE DISNEY ICE PRINCESS AND
LET IT GO.

WHEN TROUBLE COMES,
THE GOOD NEWS IS THAT
NOW THE TWO OF YOU CAN
FACE THE CHALLENGE TOGETHER.

ONE OF THE TOUGHEST
TRANSITIONS IN MARRIAGE IS FROM
"MINE" TO "OURS."
MARRIAGE EXPOSES OUR
INNATE SELFISHNESS.

INSIDE JOKES
ARE ROCKET FUEL
TO A RELATIONSHIP.
FIND OUT WHAT'S FUNNY
JUST TO THE TWO OF YOU.
THE NEXT TIME IT HAPPENS
AT A BORING DINNER PARTY,
YOU CAN DO THE
RAISED-EYEBROWS GLANCE
AT EACH OTHER AND
TRY NOT TO LAUGH.

WHEN THINGS GO SIDEWAYS,
DON'T SAY EVERYTHING
THAT POPS IN YOUR MIND.
IT'S HUMAN NATURE:
THE MADDER YOU GET,
THE LESS YOU USE A FILTER.
JUST BECAUSE YOU THINK IT
DOESN'T MEAN YOU
NEED TO SAY IT.

FIND WAYS TO
LAUGH TOGETHER.
THERE IS TRULY SOMETHING MAGICAL
ABOUT LAUGHING AT THE SAME
THING AT THE SAME TIME.

FIND PEOPLE WHO MAKE YOUR MARRIAGE BETTER. PEOPLE YOU CAN LEARN FROM AND BE ENCOURAGED BY.

YOU NEED TO BE AROUND COUPLES WHO BRING YOU CLOSER RATHER THAN BRINGING YOU DRAMA.

SOMEWHERE DEEP IN YOUR BRAIN,
YOU PROBABLY ARE FORMULATING A
LIST OF PET PEEVES ABOUT YOUR SPOUSE,
LIKE CRACKING KNUCKLES OR LEAVING
SOCKS ON THE BEDROOM FLOOR.

THAT'S NOT FAIR.

YOUR SPOUSE WILL NEVER KNOW WHAT BUGS
YOU IF YOU KEEP THIS LIST BURIED IN YOUR
BRAIN AND NEVER SAY ANYTHING.
(AND WHAT IF YOU NOT TELLING THEM THINGS
THAT BUG YOU IS ON THEIR PET-PEEVES LIST?)

LIFE CAN BE REALLY HARD.
WHAT IS ONE TANGIBLE,
UNEXPECTED THING
YOU CAN DO TODAY
TO MAKE LIFE
**A TINY BIT EASIER
FOR YOUR SPOUSE?**

WHEN YOU ARE
TALKING OR FUSSING
OR (ESPECIALLY) SIX-ALARM ARGUING,
LOOK FOR COMMON GROUND.
WORK TO UNDERSTAND EACH OTHER,
NOT TO WIN A FIGHT.

PUT YOUR PHONES AWAY AT LEAST ONE NIGHT A WEEK.

THE MINUTE THE WORKDAY ENDS,
THE PHONES GO IN THE DRAWER
UNTIL THE ALARM RINGS
THE NEXT MORNING.

ATTACK THE PROBLEM, NOT EACH OTHER. YOU OR YOUR SPOUSE IS RARELY (IF EVER) THE ISSUE. **TRY TO UNDERSTAND** EACH OTHER'S PERSPECTIVE AND FIND A SOLUTION THAT WORKS FOR BOTH OF YOU.

CELEBRATE YOUR FAMILY'S WINS,

BIG OR SMALL.

LET THESE CELEBRATIONS

BECOME PART OF THE RHYTHM

OF YOUR RELATIONSHIP.

IT'S NOT A GOOD IDEA
TO COMPARE YOUR
ENTIRE MARRIAGE
(THE GOOD, THE BAD, AND THE UGLY)
WITH SOMEBODY ELSE'S
FILTERED SNAPSHOT.

DON'T WITHHOLD FORGIVENESS
FROM YOUR SPOUSE.
**DON'T MAKE IT CONDITIONAL
OR TEMPORARY OR PARTIAL
OR DEPENDENT.
SIMPLY FORGIVE.**

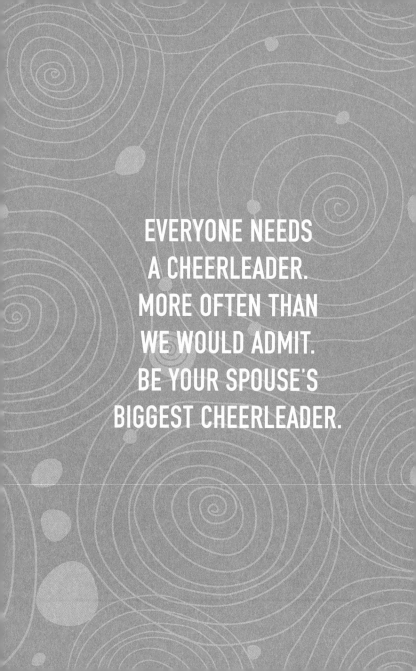

EVERYONE NEEDS
A CHEERLEADER.
MORE OFTEN THAN
WE WOULD ADMIT.
BE YOUR SPOUSE'S
BIGGEST CHEERLEADER.

THE FIRST YEAR OF
MARRIAGE HAS BEEN
COMPARED TO
WET CEMENT.
SMOOTH OUT THE ROUGH
SPOTS BEFORE THEY HARDEN.

DON'T FILL A FILING CABINET FULL
OF FRUSTRATIONS AND THEN
DUMP THEM ON YOUR SPOUSE
ALL AT ONCE.
IT'S REALLY UNFAIR,
AND THE CLEANUP
IS NO FUN.

SOMETIMES YOU JUST
HOLD HANDS AND CRY.
THAT'S OKAY.

LOVE IS NOT
JUST A FEELING.
LOVE IS A CHOICE.
THERE WILL BE DAYS
WHEN YOUR FEELINGS
DO NOT MATCH YOUR LOVE.
THAT'S OKAY, BUT MAKE
SURE YOU ALWAYS
CHOOSE LOVE.